14 LESSONS I LEARNED FROM HEART SURGERY

by

Roger L. Alford

COPYRIGHT 2019 by Roger L. Alford

Published by Kennedy Publishing Group
Granbury, TX- United States of America
All Rights Reserved 2019
ISBN-9781793935489

Scripture quotations from The Authorized (King James) Version. Rights in the Authorized Version in the United Kingdom are vested in the Crown. Reproduced by permission of the Crown's patentee, Cambridge University Press. Scripture taken from the HOLY BIBLE, NEW INTERNATIONAL VERSION®. Copyright© 1973, 1978, 1984 by International Bible Society. Used by permission of Zondervan. All rights reserved.

Scripture quotations marked (TLB) are taken from The Living Bible copyright © 1971. Used by permission of Tyndale House Publishers, Inc., Carol Stream, Illinois 60188. All rights reserved.
No part of this book may be reproduced or transmitted in any form without written permission from the author.

PREFACE

Most Christians believe God can do anything, but very few actually believe Him when they are in the fire. Yet, it is in the fiery furnace that God's grace becomes most evident. My good friend and brother in Christ, Minister Roger Alford can attest to that first hand. During his heart attack and subsequent heart surgery, he experienced the Lord's sustaining grace to endure the hardness and overcome a whole range of human emotions. Sure the pain was real and the negative thoughts and feelings were intense, but our Lord's marvelous presence, peace and provision for all of Roger's needs were far greater.

"Lessons from Heart Surgery" contains valuable testimonies that will encourage and equip you for whatever difficulties you may encounter. As Roger was sharing with me what he learned during this challenging time, I kept thinking that this could help a lot of people and he should put them in a book. I am so glad he did! We all need to know that the Lord is real and that He will sustain us through our trials. You will greatly benefit from reading "lessons from Heart Surgery" because the lessons hold true in every situation.

Dr. Lewis Gregory[1],
President of Source Ministries International
Atlanta, GA
08/03/2018

INTRODUCTION

Recently I was sitting in my recliner watching TV and all of a sudden a severe pain shot down my left arm. My chest became heavy, and I broke out in a cold sweat. My breathing got shallow. Uh oh, I recognized signs of a heart attack! I asked my wife to call 911. They confirmed it - a heart attack. After testing me, I thought the doctor would put in a stent. Instead he said I needed triple bypass surgery.

This all came as a shock to me; for I thought I was in perfect health. I didn't smoke, drink, or use drugs. I wasn't overweight and I exercised regularly and tried to eat right. I was not stressed out and had peace of mind. So this came as a surprise to me and to all who knew me. They thought I'd be the last person in the world to need heart surgery. It just goes to show you how life can sneak up on you. Things can change overnight.

I am thankful to all the folks who prayed for me, sent messages, called, visited, and supported me and my dear wife. God has been very gracious to us.

But even in the midst of such a trial, God taught me some valuable lessons. So, I want to share them with you. Whether you have to go through heart surgery or any such trial, I hope these lessons enlighten and encourage you.

LESSON #1

I now appreciate more the little things: like the taste of food, seeing God's beautiful creation like trees and flowers, feeling the warm sun and fresh breeze on your face, hearing the birds. I no longer want to take for granted a few hours of sleep, being pain free, being able to walk without someone having to steady me and a host of other little things of every day.

LESSON #2

If our trust is in God, we have nothing to fear. I have preached that for years and this experience proved that to be true. I knew I was having the symptoms of a heart attack, but I was not afraid. We called 911 and as the EMT's checked me out-no fear... As the doctor told me he needed to cut my chest open- no fear... When I woke up from surgery- no fear. I felt the presence of Jesus through it all, as my closest Friend. So His promise proved to be true that He would never leave me nor forsake me, therefore we have nothing to fear. Been there, done that, and got the t-shirt (actually an 8" scar!)

LESSON #3

Share your story. I have been enlightened by the testimonies of others who have been through this, or who are presently going through it. We all have some experience in life that can benefit someone else going through the same. So share your story with someone so they can be encouraged, find hope, and be built up in Faith. It will bless them as I have been blessed.

LESSON #4

God's timing is perfect. Now I understand better why I had not been able to make earlier connections for upcoming mission trips out of the country. God knew this was coming and was protecting me from the heart attack happening in a foreign country. Those trips can come in the future. Even though I could not go to Juarez, Mexico to train 30 pastors, I was able to ship them 30 copies of my book that I would have taught from! God is never early and never late. He knows what He is doing.

LESSON #5

Realize the impact from the support and love from friends and family. It has been so good to receive phone calls, texts, emails, cards, visits, meals, money, reading material, a car wash, smiles, hugs, (just not too hard), a verse of Scripture and most of all prayers. And it has been a blessing to see people also support my wife in many ways. One of my favorite sayings is: "If you love me, tell me now; I can't hear you when I'm dead!" Now I will make a more concerted effort to not just say I love someone, but to find a tangible way to show it! Jesus didn't just say He loves me; He died on a cross in my place!

LESSON #6

God showed me I'm not indispensable, and He can do His work with or without me. I felt like a dot in the ocean. The world kept going on without me. No matter what shape I'm in, Almighty God is still on the throne! It's all up to Him. However, He chooses to use human instruments like me. Since I am still alive, He obviously still has a plan for me here on Earth!

LESSON #7

I did not mind that I was not connected to social media - phone, texts, emails, TV, radio, etc. I didn't really care about the latest news on Washington, or President Trump[2], or North Korea (as if I could change any of that anyhow). I didn't care about the stock market, the weather (whether it was hot or cold, or rainy or clear). I didn't care what anyone was wearing, including the hospital gown I was wearing. It didn't matter if their hair was a mess or my hair both (I needed a haircut before the surgery, and Elaine said my hair was sticking out like Bozo the Clown[3]). I was unshaven and looked a mess, but I was in "survival mode". To "survive" means to manage to keep going in spite of difficult circumstances. I was just seeking to take a deep breath without feeling like I had a knife in my chest. Boy, do we ever complain a lot about stuff that has nothing to do with survival. But even in the midst of just "surviving", I was at the same time "more than a conqueror." The Bible says in *Romans 8:35 "Who shall separate us from the love of Christ? Shall trouble or hardship or persecution or famine or nakedness (no modesty in the hospital) or danger or sword?"* And may I add "or heart surgery"? And verse 37: *"No, in all these things we are more than conquerors through Him who loved us!"*

LESSON #8

A few months ago my missionary friend Lewis Gregory felt impressed by God to send me a warning (a prophecy) that contained three points.

1. "You are going to be sifted." This is what Christ told Peter in Luke 22:31. Little did neither he nor I know it would be open heart surgery! Talk about sifting!

2. "It will not be your fault." It wasn't like I had not been taking care of my body. I was in great shape for a 70 year old. Often people think that when something bad happens to you, you must be at fault or have sin in your life.

3. "God will use this to teach you some new things and expand your ministry." Well, friends, these very lessons you are now reading

are some of the new things I've learned and am now experiencing. And I can hardly wait to see my ministry expanding... for His glory!

So to sum up Lesson #8: God knows what is ahead, and He prepares you for it, and sees you through it, and teaches you wonderful things, and uses you on the other side of it. Our God reigns!

LESSON #9

I have learned to pray more for others who are suffering. I realize that my problems are not nearly as big as some other folks'. But I can now empathize more with people who can hardly sleep at night, who have no appetite, who can't taste good food, who are in pain or can't get comfortable, who have little energy, or even worse. I pray every time I hear the siren of an ambulance for God to have mercy on that person as I now know what it's like to be carried in one.

But most of all I now appreciate even more the suffering Jesus went through for me as He endured the excruciating pain and agony on the cross. And He didn't have to, but out of love and compassion for me and you He paid the penalty for our sins, Oh, what a Savior!

LESSON #10

I have experienced firsthand how God uses people He has given medical knowledge to know how to help folks. I'm referring to doctors, nurses, lab techs, radiologists, anesthesiologists, druggists, chemists and medical scientists, researchers, physical therapists, home health aides, EMTs, dietitians, orderlies, etc. I have learned to appreciate these folks more than ever. They have benefitted me greatly! I appreciate that they studied and trained to help people like me. But the knowledge they obtained did not originate from man but from God. All truth comes from God. *"Jesus is the way, the truth and the life" - John: 14:6*. This includes all medical truth (knowledge). *Proverbs 2:6 says, "For the Lord gives wisdom: out of*

His mouth comes knowledge and understanding."

Many people pray and ask God to help them, He can do it by a supernatural miracle, or He may choose to use those medical practitioners to whom He has already given the knowledge on how to help you. Either way, God should get the credit and the glory!

LESSON #11

I have a new appreciation of how much others mean to me. When I got to thinking I may never see them again, I realized how easy it was to take them for granted (to expect them to always be available or to value them too lightly). This applies to friends and family especially my wife Elaine. I'm more grateful now for her unconditional love, devotion, and service to me. She has unselfishly sacrificed time and sleep to nurse me back to health. Add to that, the care offered me by my children, friends and acquaintances, I am a blessed man. Thank God for the people God has put in your life, and look at them with a new appreciation, as if you may never see them again!

LESSON #12

I am so glad that I had memorized some Bible verses over the years. As I lay in ICU, I had no access to a Bible, nor was I in shape to read one. But God brought to my remembrance some Scriptures that helped me make it through: for instance when I had a rough time sleeping at night - *Psalm 127:2 - "God gives sleep to those He loves."* And I also remembered *Romans 8:28 - "All things work together for good for those who love Him."* Even if it didn't feel good or look good, I knew He was in charge! To sum up this lesson: Since childhood I had learned these verses and now could pull them to the forefront of my mind. *Psalm 119:11 KJV - "Thy word have I hid in my heart that I might not sin against Thee."* Therefore I did not have to fall into fear, despair, mistrust, anxiety, frustration, discouragement, depression, or worry. Full of pain, discomfort, and an unknown future I claimed *Ephesians 2:14: "Jesus is our peace"!* So invest time in God's Word, and later you will reap great dividends!

LESSON #13

God supplies my needs, even though I have not been able to work. One thought that crossed my mind right after surgery was "How am I going to make it financially until I recuperate and get back to working (preaching and mission work)?" To a large extent our livelihood depends on love offerings (donations to our ministry). I wondered if it would be a case of "out of sight, out of mind." But we are never out of God's sight nor off His mind! I have learned afresh that God still works today like He did for Abraham in the Bible: "God is my provider." When things happen outside of our control, like a heart attack, our part is to continue to trust and obey Him. Where God leads, God feeds. Where God guides, God provides!

LESSON #14

It was very important to me to know that, whether I made it through the surgery or not, I knew that I would go to Heaven when I die. It is vital to be ready to face death whenever it may come. I realized I was only a heartbeat away from eternity. Actually we all are. Do you know for sure that you will go to Heaven when you die? You can know, according to the Bible. *1st John 5:13 says, "I write these things to you who believe in the name of the Son of God so you may know that you have eternal life."* To believe in Jesus is not just some mental acknowledgement that He exists - even the devil knows that. To believe in Jesus means to believe that He is the Son of God who died on the cross in your place, as payment for your sins. It includes putting your trust in Him for the salvation of your soul and trusting Him to take you to Heaven when you die. You must open the door of your heart and invite Him to come in, save you, and take control of your life. If you do that, then you have truly believed in Him; i.e., put your faith in Him as your only hope for eternal life, and now you can know that you are ready to face death.

CONCLUSION:

As time goes on, I'm sure I will continue to learn even more lessons. There's an old saying, "You can't teach an old dog new tricks". Well, I am not a dog, so I am open to learning more new things from God.

To sum up, I see each new day as a present from God. And I look forward to however He may use me in the future. As the Apostle Paul said in *Philippians 1:21-25 (Living Bible translation) "For to me, living means opportunities for Christ, and dying - well, that's better yet! But if living will give me more opportunities to win people to Christ, then I really don't know which is better, to live or die! Sometimes I want to live and other times I don't, for I long to go and be with Christ. How much happier for me than being here! But the fact is that I can be of more help to you by staying! Yes, I am still needed down here so I feel certain I will be staying on earth a little longer, to help you grow and become happy in your faith."*

References

1. Dr. Lewis Gregory-is the Director of Source Ministries International. His responsibilities include teaching, preaching, counseling and writing. He is personally committed to the ministry of life and the encouragement of others. (Excerpts used with permission from Dr. Lewis Gregory's book-The New You-Preview, August 2018)
Source Ministries International, Inc.
www.sourceministries.net

2. President Donald Trump-
Donald John Trump is the 45th President of the United States of America.

3. **Bozo the Clown-** is a fictional clown character created by Alan W. Livingston and introduced in 1946 and to television in 1949.

About the Author:

Roger Alford has pastored over 40 years in churches in Texas, Kentucky, Missouri and Kansas. He has preached revivals and led pastor's conferences in several states and foreign nations. He and his wife Elaine have three children and eleven grandchildren. Roger can be contacted at:
www.newfaithministries.net

Other books by Roger Alford:

Pastoring Isn't All It's
Cracked Up To Be... It's More!

PASTOREAR
NO ES LO QUE PARECE SER
ES MAS!

Made in the USA
Columbia, SC
11 March 2019